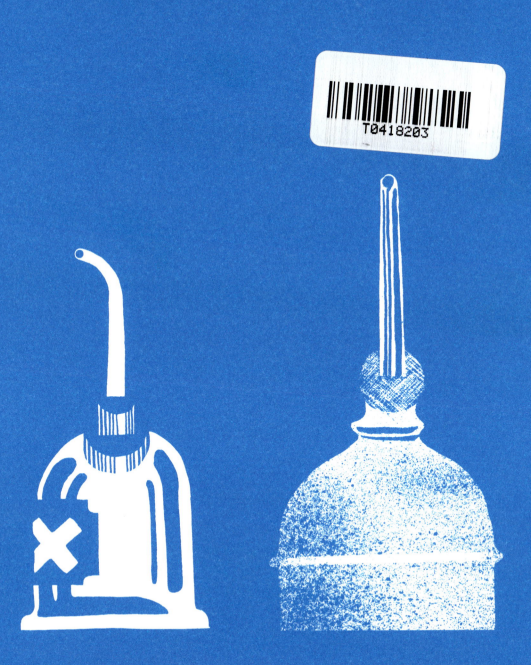

Meet the Typographer
Written and illustrated by Gaby Bazin

Published by
David Zwirner Books
520 West 20th Street, 2nd Floor
New York, New York 10011
+ 1 212 727 2070
davidzwirnerbooks.com

Editor: Jessica Palinski Hoos
Proofreader: Chris Peterson
Translator: Vineet Lal
Printer: PBtisk
Typeface: Nanami Rounded Pro
Paper: Munken Print Cream 150 gsm

Publication © 2025 David Zwirner Books
Text and illustrations © 2022 Éditions MeMo
Translation © 2024 Vineet Lal
First published in 2022 in French by Éditions MeMo

For their expert advice and assistance, the translator and David Zwirner Books would like to thank
Richard Ardagh, New North Press; Christopher Barker, The Smallprint Company;
Claire and David Bolton, The Alembic Press; Alicia Chilcott, Bob Richardson and the team, St Bride Foundation;
Jack Conkie, Robert Smail's Printing Works, in the care of the National Trust for Scotland;
Justin Knopp, Typoretum; Evgenia Kochkina, Stoneberry Press; Ambre Morvan; Graham Moss, Incline Press;
Lisa Paice, Lyme Bay Press; Joe Pearson, Design For Today; Christine Penman; and Simon Russell.

All rights reserved. No part of this book may be reproduced or transmitted in any form or
by any means, electronic or mechanical, including photographing, recording, or
information storage and retrieval, without prior permission in writing from the publisher.

Distributed in the United States and Canada by
Simon & Schuster, Inc.
1230 Avenue of the Americas
New York, New York 10020
simonandschuster.com

Distributed outside the United States, United Kingdom, and Canada by
Thames & Hudson, Ltd.
181A High Holborn
London WC1V 7QX
thamesandhudson.com

ISBN: 978-1-64423-157-9
Library of Congress Control Number: 2024941503

Printed in the Czech Republic

Written and illustrated by Gaby Bazin

Translated by Vineet Lal

David Zwirner Books

Welcome to my studio!

Let's find out about letterpress printing and the art of the typographer.

Here, you'll discover a craft that has existed for more than five hundred years.

I create books and posters, thanks to individual letter blocks, called movable type, and enormous printing machines, called presses.

Don't worry, I'll show you how it all works!

A long, long time before printing presses, and even longer before computers and photocopiers, there were no machines capable of duplicating a text.

It had to be copied, patiently, by hand.

In Mesopotamia, for example, people wrote with a stylus on soft clay tablets.

In Egypt, they would use a reed pen—made by cutting the tip of a reed at an angle—to write on sheets of papyrus.

In India, people turned to palm leaves they could write on with ink or inscribe with a pointed stylus.

In East Asia, they preferred the softness of a fine paintbrush and silk.

The Greeks and the Romans, for their part, would write on wax tablets.

In the Middle Ages, in Europe, people used goose quills to create their manuscripts.

This work was so time-consuming and tedious that books could cost a fortune and the scribes occasionally made mistakes.

In the fifteenth century, in northern Europe, people began to engrave both words and images together on pieces of wood. They would spread ink over these engravings to make a print.

But carving so many tiny letters, or characters, one by one, was an incredibly long and painstaking task.

In China, in the eleventh century, the artisan Pi Sheng had the idea to cut away at little clay blocks, leaving each character in relief.

That's how the first movable type was born.

Apparently unaware of this invention in China, a German goldsmith set out to make solid movable type from metal. He worked at this for many long years.

Inspired by the presses winegrowers used to crush grapes, he also constructed an imposing-looking machine: the printing press.

He even developed a thick, paste-like ink that transferred easily from the type to the page.

And so Johannes Gutenberg became known as the father of my craft: letterpress printing.

This is the system Gutenberg devised to make movable type from lead:

First the letter is cut, in relief, into the end of a short piece of hard metal. The letter must be back to front.

This is called a punch.

The punch is used to strike a bar of softer metal, leaving an impression of the letter behind. The letter is now the right way around.

This is called a matrix.

The matrix is placed in a mould that is then filled with molten lead.

The result is a block of metal type ready to be typeset into words. The letter is reversed again, but it will print the right way around, just like a rubber stamp would.

This process must be repeated many times to produce multiple copies of all the characters:

capital (or uppercase) letters,

small (or lowercase) letters,

accents, special characters,

numbers,

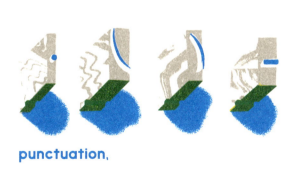

punctuation,

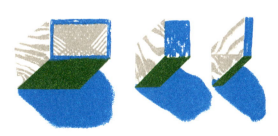

and even the spaces that separate words!

All the hard work required did not discourage Gutenberg, who set out to create his first book.

Around 1455, he completed his legendary forty-two-line Bible, which contains more than a thousand pages of densely packed text.

As printers are known to say, "'Tis a thing of beauty!"

The type crafted by Gutenberg imitated the style of quill writing common in Germany at the time.

Since then, typography has come a long way, and now we can choose between all sorts of typefaces:

blackletter

rounded

CONDENSED

bold

script

serif

or sans serif.

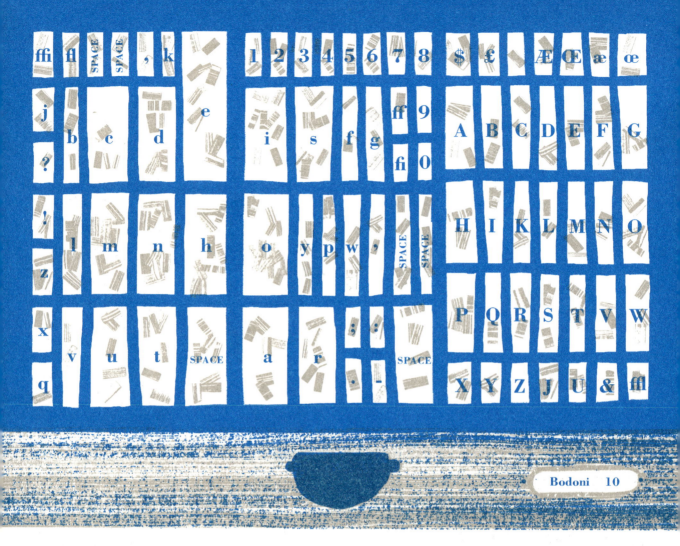

Within a case, the type lives in a series of little compartments, sometimes called boxes. The characters that are used most often are in the middle, while the rest are around the sides.

Capitals—which are used less frequently—are often kept in a separate case, above the small letters. That's where the terms "uppercase" and "lowercase" come from! This type case combines both capital and small letters, all from the same font.

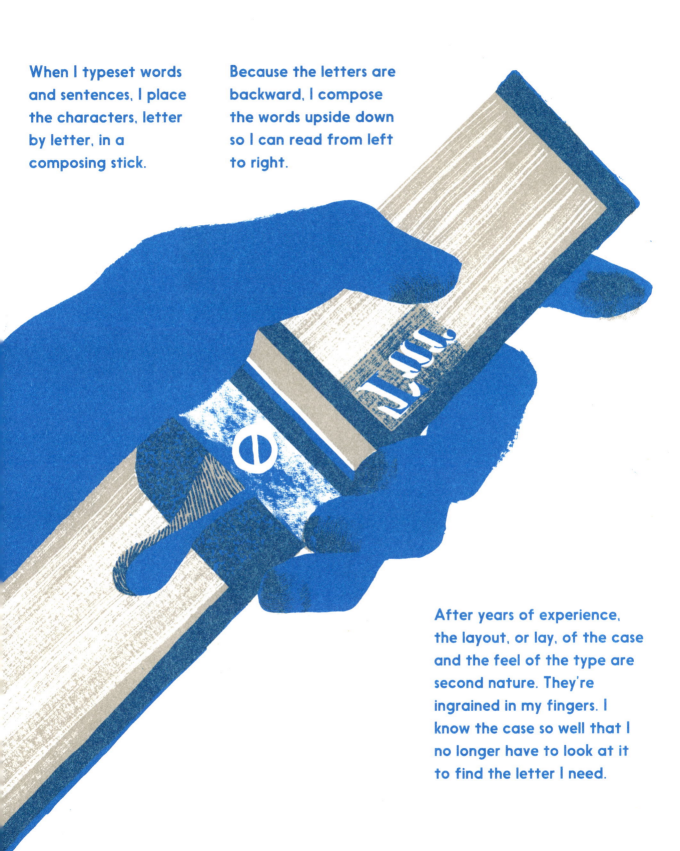

When I typeset words and sentences, I place the characters, letter by letter, in a composing stick.

Because the letters are backward, I compose the words upside down so I can read from left to right.

After years of experience, the layout, or lay, of the case and the feel of the type are second nature. They're ingrained in my fingers. I know the case so well that I no longer have to look at it to find the letter I need.

Now then, make yourself useful by checking this word in a mirror.

Goodness me, you're right. Some scatterbrain must have mixed up the letters "u" and "n."

Look, it's much better like this, isn't it?

Let me put together a few lines of text to show you how fast I am.

Speed is key in composing type! In fact, in printers' slang in France, the person who does the typesetting— the typesetter or compositor—was sometimes nicknamed "the monkey."

It's true that, with time, typographers become as nimble as spider monkeys.

There you go: I'm done. The lines are stacked on top of one another. To hold them securely, I tie them up, nice and tight, like a Sunday roast.

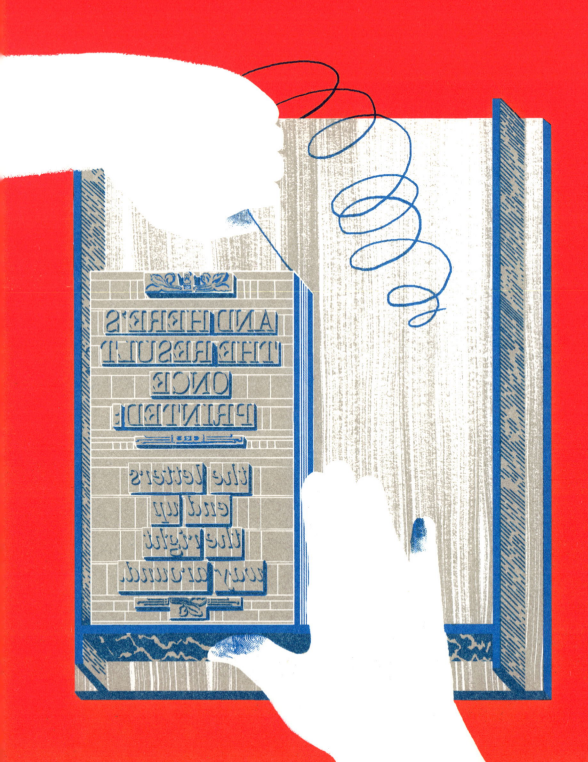

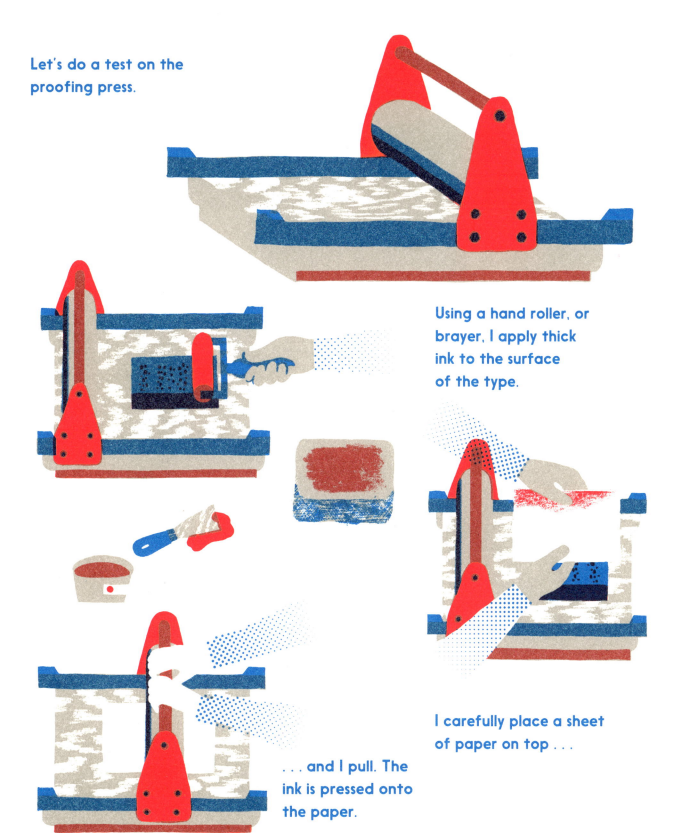

Here's the inked-up type:

AND HERE'S THE RESULT ONCE PRINTED:

the letters end up the right way around.

I don't mean to boast, but I usually take on far more complex projects. Whole books, for example!

These days, there are much faster ways to print. I, however, produce only special, high-quality pieces of work.

The job isn't finished yet!

Now I'm off to clean my tools, tidy away the little characters, and take care of my beloved presses.

Right then, I don't want to
rush you, but I've got three
books that should have been
printed yesterday . . .

It was great to see you.
Bye for now, little monkey!

quoin and quoin key

planer

mallet

brush

ink knife

hand roller/brayer

inks